# THE ROYAL
# CATHEDRAL
# AT WAWEL HILL

*To the memory of*
*Fr Kazimierz Figlewicz*

KRZYSZTOF J. CZYŻEWSKI

# THE ROYAL CATHEDRAL AT WAWEL HILL
## GUIDEBOOK

Photographs:

**ADAM BUJAK**

ST STANISLAUS BISHOP MARTYR PUBLISHING HOUSE
Archdiocese of Cracow
Kraków 2001

Typeset by Adam Urbanik

Translated by Katarzyna Mroczkowska
and Jadwiga Piątkowska

*The photograph artist Adam Bujak offered gratuitously*
*his photographs and his assistance to this guidebook,*
*contributing to the restoration of Wawel Cathedral.*

© Wydawnictwo św. Stanisława BM
31-101 Kraków, ul. Straszewskiego 2
tel. +48 (012) 429 52 17, fax +48 (012) 421 49 70
e-mail: wydawnictwo@diecezja.krakow.pl

**ISBN 83-87960-76-4**

Printed by:
PLATAN

*In the name of God,*
  *I greet visitors to the Cathedral!*

+ Rancinch kad. Macharh—

# BRIEF HISTORY
# OF WAWEL CATHEDRAL

**T**he first cathedral on Wawel Hill was erected most probably soon after the establishment of the Cracow bishopric in 1000. Unfortunately, the archaeological research carried out so far has not yielded results which would allow for reconstructing its appearance. The next cathedral, Romanesque in style, came into being at the turn of the 11th and 12th centuries. The beginning of its construction is usually associated with the reign of Prince Ladislaus Herman (1079-1102), that is why it is often called Herman's cathedral. The consecration of the church built of limestone blocks and sandstone ashlars took place in 1142. It was a three-aisle basilica (probably with galleries), with two rectangular choirs with semicircular apses (at both the east and west ends), and with crypts underneath the choirs. The interior was probably vaulted. Two square towers flanked the west front. Substantial parts of the Romanesque structure, such as St.Leonard's Crypt and the lower section of the south tower, have survived to the present day. We know relatively little about the interior decorations, in terms of architecture and sculpture, but inventories made and written down in 1101 and 1110 testify to the richness of the furnishings kept in the cathedral treasury, and to the wealth of the library.

**C**racow Cathedral was the centre of the cult of St Stanislaus, Bishop of Cracow, canonized in 1253. Pilgrims from Poland, as well as from the neighbouring countries, journeyed to his tomb. The cult of St. Stanislaus was connected with the idea of unifying the Kingdom of Poland, broken up into provinces, so it is not surprising that, contrary to the previous tradition of crowning kings in the cathedral of Gniezno, the Archbishop's see, the coronation of Ladislaus the Short was held in Cracow Cathedral on the 20th of January 1320, next to the relics of the patron saint of the reborn Polish monarchy. From then on, Wawel Cathedral became the place of coronation of the kings of Poland.

**T**he Romanesque cathedral (damaged by time and the fire of 1305) was replaced with the new Gothic one (preserved almost intact to the present day), erected in stages from 1320 to 1346 (the presbytery and ambulatory), and from 1346 to 1364 (the nave). Several different mason workshops were employed in turn on the construction of the cathedral. Its consecration took place on the 28th March 1364.

The Gothic cathedral was a three-aisle basilica with a transept and a rectangular presbytery with an ambulatory. The cathedral is surprisingly small in size, but owing to its artistic value, its well-developed spatial plan and rich interior architectural decorations, it occupies an important place in the history of Gothic architecture in Central Europe.

**A**lready when the church was being constructed, bishops and magnates built the first chapels as surrounding it. This continued through the 14th and 15th c. The chapels founded by the monarchs were most remarkable because of their grand and sumptuous form. They were the chapels built by King Casimir the Great (Chapel of the Assumption of the BVM); Queen Sophia, the fourth wife of King Ladislaus Jagiełło (Chapel of the Holy Trinity); and king Casimir IV and his wife Elizabeth of Austria (Chapel of the Holy Cross and the Holy Spirit).

**I**n the late Middle Ages and the early 16th c. the interior of the cathedral contained many altars, varied in shape, painted and sculpted. There were twenty three of them, apart from those in the chapels and in St Leonard's Crypt. All of them were sumptuously furnished with liturgical paraphernalia kept in special cupboards and chests. Apart from the High Altar and the Sacrament house (where the Holy Sacrament was kept), the most prominent was the altar of St Stanislaus, placed in the centre of the church, next to the screen between the nave and the presbytery, which was reserved for the clergy. At the top of the screen was the figure of Christ Crucified, which expressed the fundamental Christian truth about Salvation, performed through the Passion and Death of the Saviour pon the cross.

The cathedral also functioned as a necropolis. To commemorate the places where kings, bishops and magnates were buried, memorial plaques were set in the floor, or grand tombs were erected. Particularly impressive are the Gothic royal tombs, admirable for their artistic quality as well as the religious and political message expressed in their shape and decoration.

It would be difficult to describe in detail the cathedral's only partially preserved medieval interior decorations, but it seems necessary to point out how colourful this interior must have been, since it contained, among other things, wall paintings, stained glass windows, glazed floor tiles, rich hangings and tapestries periodically hung up on the walls. To complete the picture, a mention must be made of the Cathedral Treasury and the Chapter Library, both containing many items impressive by their number and quality.

The 16th c. brought major changes in the style of the cathedral's interior decorations. The beginnings of the Renaissance in the cathedral (as well as in all of Poland) are connected with the activity of Francesco of Florence, the artist who created the tomb of King John Albert (d.1501). But the real breakthrough came when the Royal Chapel (known today as the Sigismund Chapel) was erected by a team of Italian artists, who executed the design by Bartolomeo Berrecci, commissioned by King Sigismund I the Elder. This chapel became the model for numerous Renaissance and Mannerist mausoleums of bishops (the chapels of Tomicki, Maciejowski, Zebrzydowski, Padniewski), built

in the cathedral to replace the older Gothic chapels. Some of the medieval altars, including the High Altar, gave place to new Renaissance ones. Many new tombs and epitaphs appeared in the 16th c., erected mostly for kings and bishops. The Renaissance and Mannerist decorations were mainly the work of outstanding artists, such as the above mentioned Bartolomeo Berrecci, Giovanni Maria Padovano, Jan Michałowicz of Urzędowo or Santi Gucci, mostly Italians who settled in Poland. Remarkable are also fine works imported to Cracow: metalwork (tombs, grilles), goldwork (part of the Sigismund Chapel furnishings) as well as painting (altar panels in the Sigismund Chapel), which were brought from Nuremberg, by such artists as Peter and Hans Vischer, Peter Flötner, Melchior Baier and Georg Pencz.

In the next two centuries the style of the cathedral interior changed considerably. In the 17th c., thanks to generous endowments coming from kings, magnates, bishops and canons, almost all furnishings dating from the previous epochs were removed, and new Mannerist and Baroque altars, tombs, stalls, paintings and other elements were introduced. Black marble from Dębnica, often inlayed with pink marble from Paczółtowice, became the typical material of this new age. As a result of the modernization of the nave and the presbytery, a new clear composition along the axis between St Stanislaus' shrine and the High Altar was created. Following the earlier tradition, new domed burial chapels (the Lipski and Zadzik's Chapels) were built. One of them was the mausoleum of the Vasa royal dynasty, which was an ideological and stylistic reference to the Sigismund Chapel. It was remarkable in copying the external shape of the Renaissance chapel built over a century earlier.

The modifications undertaken in the 18th c. transformed the style of the cathedral's interior into the late-Baroque. The interior decorations which so far had been quite diverse in terms of shape, material and type of ornaments, were replaced by new ones in most cases, as well as arranged in an orderly way, unified following the rules of symmetry, and organized along the clear composition axes. The number of side altars was considerably reduced.

As in the previous centuries, new domed mausoleums were erected (the chapel of the Lipski family and Załuski's Chapel). However, the next royal chapel which was to commemorate the Saxon Wettin dynasty remained only a project. Fortunately, the basic Gothic architectural structure of the cathedral was not essentially modified (as was the case of the cathedrals in Gniezno and Poznań). Nor was the project of erecting a neoclassical west front realized. Yet regretfully, in order to provide for the best possible illumination of the interior, the walls of the ambulatory were raised to the height of the presbytery, thus changing the spatial composition and the shape of the east end of the church.

Nonetheless, it should be pointed out that the Baroque interior of the cathedral was, in most part, the work of outstanding Italian artists (Giovanni Trevano, Giovanni Battista Gisleni and Francesco Placidi), or artists educated in Italy (Kacper Bażanka).

Poland's loss of independence, the time of the Partitions, negatively influenced also the condition of Cracow Cathedral. The royal endowments ceased, the once extremely rich Chapter landed property was cut down to a minimum, and did not allow either to maintain the cathedral on a proper level or to modernize it on such a scale as in the previous centuries. Nevertheless, some of the chapels and monuments were renovated in the 19th c. As modern theories of art conservation appeared and developed, some of the activities undertaken in the cathedral were discussed and critically assessed.

Research in the field of historical sciences (including the new discipline of art history), the development of national consciousness and, in the face of the country's loss of independence, a need for bringing back the memory of the times of Poland's greatness, increased the awareness that Wawel Cathedral, the place of the Polish kings' coronation and the royal necropolis, was of enormous significance in historical, artistic and emotional terms. It became the object of patriotic pilgrimages and the venue for celebrating anniversaries of major events in Poland's history. Of crucial importance was the burial in the crypts of Wawel Cathedral of Poland's spiritual leader, the poet Adam Mickiewicz, and of national heroes (Tadeusz Kościuszko, Józef Poniatowski), who had fought for the freedom of the country. Thus Wawel cathedral became the Polish Pantheon where only the most worthy Poles could be buried. This tradition was continued in the 20th c. when Juliusz Słowacki, Józef

Piłsudski and Władysław Sikorski were laid to rest in the cathedral.

As for new works of art which in the 19th c. enriched the artistic heritage of the past, it is worth pointing out the group of neoclassical monuments executed in the renowned studios of Florence and Rome. In this group the sculptures of Bertel Thorvaldsen come to the fore. Thanks to the initiative of Zofia Potocka, the last domed burial chapel in the cathedral was created. It is neoclassical in style, and could be called an artistic import, since the designer and most of the artists and craftsmen were brought from abroad. The chapel founded by Anna Wąsowicz (the remodelled medieval chapel of the Holy Trinity) had a different character, as it was designed in the neo-Gothic style, perfectly corresponding with the romantic period.

The Cathedral Treasury, even though depleted as a result of the pillage during the Swedish occupation (1655-1657), and further reduced in 1794 because its most precious valuables were donated to support the Kościuszko Insurrection, was still rich in historical items, and thus became a sort of a national museum, which was made accessible to the public in the last quarter of the 19th c. Its collection was increased not only with new vessels and liturgical vestments, but also with historical items previously kept in private collections.

The great restoration works carried out in the years 1895-1910, under the direction of Sławomir Odrzywolski and later Zygmunt Hendel, played an instrumental role in giving the cathedral its present shape. A thorough conservation of the whole edifice, together with its furnishings, was then undertaken. The historical stratification of the subsequent artistic periods was respected in principle, although some of the Baroque interior decoration was, unfortunately, removed. Some new elements were introduced, such as royal tombs (of St Jadwiga and King Ladislaus III) and monuments of bishops, new polychromy, stained glass windows, grilles, and many others. Some of these elements, in line with the then fashionable Art Nouveau forms, were works of art executed by outstanding artists, most eminent among them being Józef Mehofer. The restoration of Wawel Cathedral carried out at the turn of the 19th and 20th c. may be seen as exemplary, in keeping with the art conservation doctrine of those days.

The 20th c. has been a period of further, continuous conservation of the cathedral and the monuments contained within it. The historical process of its transformation has basically come to an end, therefore new elements of interior decorations are introduced with the greatest caution. The most recent restoration of the external elevation and the conservation of the subsequent chapels have been carried out so that the cathedral can shine with the full glamour of all its beauty in the year 2000 when the Cracow diocese celebrates its millennium.

For almost a thousand years the Cracow metropolitan basilica of St Stanislaus and St Wenceslas has been fulfilling the role of „the mother of the churches„ in one of the most important of Polish dioceses (archdiocese since 1925). The liturgy and all other forms of service performed here have always stood out as exceptionally magnificent and have been considered a model to be imitated in other churches. In its best days the cathedral had more than a hundred priests serving, saying Mass, taking part in liturgy throughout the whole day and night. The Chapter stood at the head of the cathedral hierarchy, with vicars as attendants. Services in some of the chapels were performed by specific groups of priests, and altars were attended by other specialized groups. The cathedral choir and organ music lent lustre to the liturgy. From the 17th c. there was also a vocal and instrumental music ensemble, often directed by outstanding composers (Bartłomiej Pękala or Grzegorz Gerwazy Gorczycki).

**W**awel Cathedral has played a very special role in the history of Poland and in the national consciousness of the Polish nation. For centuries it has been the place of the cult of St Stanislaus, which was strongly associated with the idea of an united and independent Polish state, the idea relevant both in the Middle Ages when Poland was divided into many provinces, and when it was partitioned in the 19th c. For centuries, St Stanislaus' tomb has been the place where trophies seized from the enemies were deposited. From the 14th to the 18th c. the cathedral was the place of the coronation and burial of the Polish monarchs. In the 19th and 20th c. it became the national Pantheon. The calling of Cardinal Karol Wojtyła, the successor of St Stanislaus, on the 16th October 1978, to St Peter's seat in Rome, can be seen as the crowning act in the history of the Cracow Diocese and its principal church. John Paul II visited what used to be his cathedral six times: in 1979, 1983, 1987, 1991, 1997, and 1999.

# WAWEL HILL

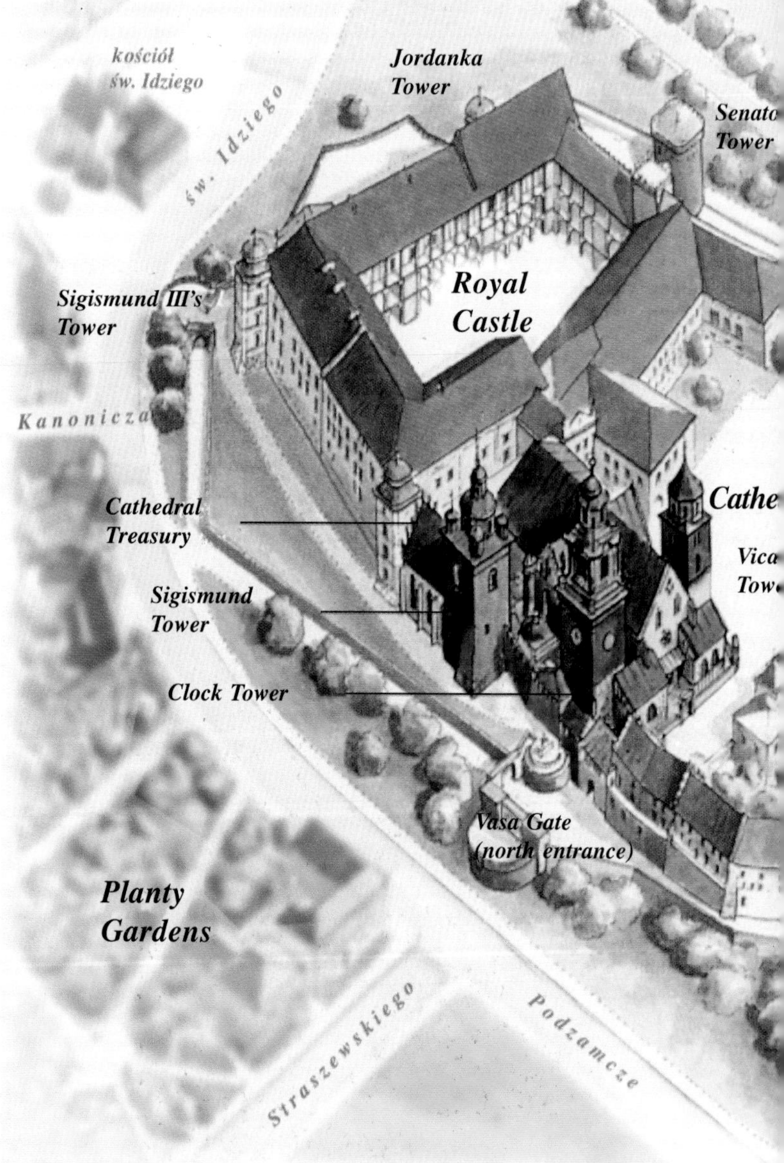

kościół
św. Idziego

Jordanka
Tower

Senato
Tower

Sigismund III's
Tower

św. Idziego

Kanonicza

Royal
Castle

Cathedral
Treasury

Cathe

Vica
Tow

Sigismund
Tower

Clock Tower

Vasa Gate
(north entrance)

Planty
Gardens

Straszewskiego

Podzamcze

# GUIDEBOOK

The cathedral is situated in the east part of Wawel Hill, at its north slope. It is approached either from Kanonicza Street, along the north elevation, or from the Bernardine Church in Stradom Street, through the Castle outer court, which provides a view of its south elevation.

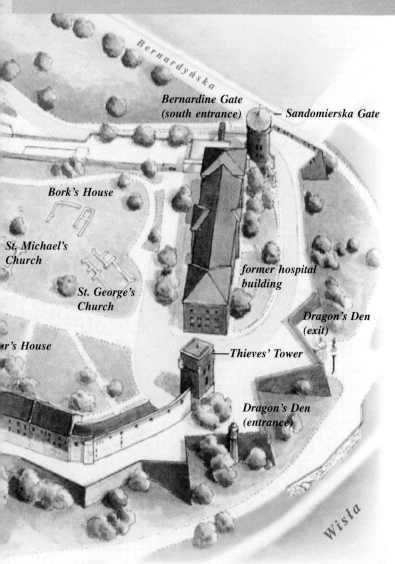

Bernardine Gate (south entrance) — Sandomierska Gate

Bork's House

St. Michael's Church

former hospital building

St. George's Church

Dragon's Den (exit)

r's House

Thieves' Tower

Dragon's Den (entrance)

Wisła

## THE NORTH ELEVATION

It is almost completely hidden by the **Gothic defensive wall**; on the inner side, adjoining to the wall, are the **buildings of the Chapterhouse, the Archive and the Chapter Library**. Aligned with the Castle walls is the **Sigismund Tower** (2nd half of the 14th c.), which was originally of defensive character, but in 1412 it became the belfry. It was repeatedly rebuilt (e.g. in 1514-1521); its present shape was established in 1897-1898 (designed by Sławomir Odrzywolski), when it was topped by the picturesque **steeple**, its shape deriving from elements of various styles. East of the tower is the **Cathedral Treasury** (built in 1481-1500 by Hanusz Blatfuss of Košice), its walls faced with limestone and decorated with the arms of the founders: Bishop Jan Rzeszowski (on the buttress finials) and Cardinal Frederick Jagiellon (the White Eagle on the gable). Above the church soars its tallest tower, first called the **Salomon Tower, and then the Clock Tower**. Its lower part has decorative stone fluting (2nd quarter of the 15th c.), and its upper brick part, built in 1518-1521 under the supervision of Canon Jan Salomon, is topped with a Baroque frieze with the arms called Pomian, and the steeple with the statues of SS Stanislaus, Adalbert, Wenceslas and Casimir; the steeple was commissioned by Bishop Kazimierz Łubieński in 1715-1716, and designed by Kacper Bażanka. The clock faces with the arms of Bishop Andrzej Trzebicki date from 1676.

## THE SOUTH ELEVATION

In the south-west corner of the cathedral is the Gothic **Vicar Tower** (also known as the **Silver Bells Tower**), built in the 14th c. above a considerable portion of the walls of the 12th –century Romanesque tower (its lower part made of limestone blocks), with the octagonal upper part, constructed in 1530 to support a late-Gothic spire modelled on the spire on the taller of the towers of St Mary's Church in Cracow, which was pulled down in 1769 and replaced with a simple tent roof. The tower contains three bells (which are often called silver bells): „Nowak" and „Goworek" (15th c.), and „Maciek" (1669, made in Gdańsk by Michał Weinhold). The **Baroque elevation of the ambulatory** was built at the time when Bishop Kazimierz Łubieński had the ambulatory extended upwards to the height of the presbytery (1713-1715, designed by Kacper Bażanka). That part of the church was different in the Middle Ages. The presbytery, with its traceried windows, supported by buttresses and flying buttresses which formed an open-work spatial structure, was topped with a frieze and a cornice with a balustrade, pinnacles and gargoyles (spouts). Numerous chapels in various styles were built along the Cathedral walls. Particularly remarkable are two chapels on both sides of the entrance in the south transept. On the right is the Renaissance **Sigismund Chapel** (1519-1553, designed by Bartolomeo Berrecci), with a dome covered with a copper roof, which was

**View of the cathedral from the south.**

# Cathedral

Clock Tower

Sigismund Tower

High Altar

Presbytery
Altar of
St Stanislaus

Nave

South Aisle

Entrance

gilded in 1591-1592, its cost covered by Queen Anne Jagiellon; it is topped with a lantern with the figure of an angel supporting a crown and a cross. The **Vasa Chapel**, on the left, is almost identical in shape, although it is much later (1664-1676, designed by Giovanni Battista Gisleni?). It provides for the symmetrical character of the south front of the cathedral but also, by repeating the form of the nearby Sigismund Chapel, it is a symbolic corroboration of the legitimacy of the Vasa dynasty on the Polish throne, as it descended in the female line (through Catherine, mother of Sigismund III) from the Jagiellonian dynasty. Among other chapels most remarkable are **three domed mausoleums** (from the left): the Mannerist Mausoleum of Bishop Filip Padniewski (1572-1575, designed by Jan Michałowicz of Urzędowo, the early-Baroque one of Bishop Jakub Zadzik (1645-1647), and the late-Baroque one of Bishop Andrzej Stanisław Kostka Załuski (1758-1766, by Francesco Placidi), topped with a cupola with the figure of a lamb with a crozier, an allusion to the founder's arms. The early-Baroque wall around the Cathedral, with three gates, was commissioned in 1619 by Bishop Piotr Tylicki (designed by Giovanni Trevano?)

## THE WEST FRONT

It is Gothic (completed c. 1364), with a triangular gable, faced with limestone blocks. Above the octagonal window is the **figure of St. Stanislaus**, the patron saint of Poland (a copy of the 14th – century statue made in 1899), and the **shield with the arms of the Kingdom of Poland**, which emphasizes the royal and national character of the cathedral, as the place of the kings' coronation and burial. The entrance is flanked by two **Gothic chapels**, their walls covered with stone fluting: on the left, the Holy Trinity Chapel (1431-1433), on the right, the Holy Cross Chapel (c.1470). Under the **coffered roof** with gilded rosettes (1643-1644) is the Baroque **portal** (1636-1637); above it is the **shield with the arms** of Bishop Bodzanta Jankowski, who completed the construction of the Gothic cathedral. In the portal is the **door** (3rd quarter of the 14th c.), covered with iron sheet, with the repeated letter K with a crown above, which was the emblem of King Casimir the Great. On both sides pof the portal are two **Gothic relief**s (c. 1320-1322), with the figures of St Margaret and St Michael the Archangel (probably details of the altar in St Margaret's Chapel, reused for the decoration of the west front.) On the wall of the Holy Trinity Chapel are suspended on a chain the **bones of Ice Age animals**, which were once considered to be the bones of the mythical dragon which had inhabited the cave in Wawel Hill. The local tradition holds that the world will continue as long as these bones hang in this particular place.

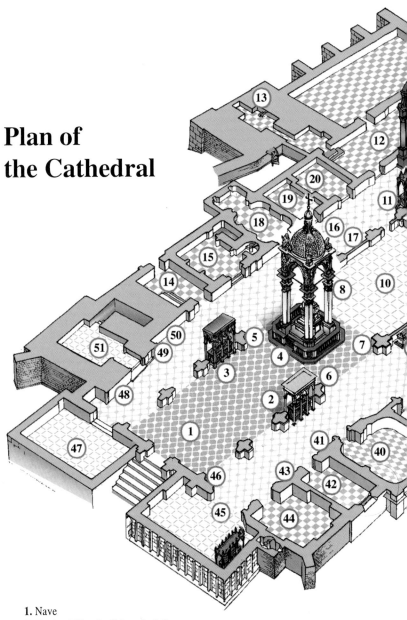

# Plan of
# the Cathedral

1. Nave
2. Tomb of King Ladislaus Jagiełło
3. Tomb of King Ladislaus III
4. Altar of St Stanislaus
5. Monument of Bishop Marcin
   Szyszkowski

6. Monument of Bishop Piotr Gembicki
7. Monument of Bishop Kazimierz
   Łubieński
8. Monument of Bishop Jan Małachowski

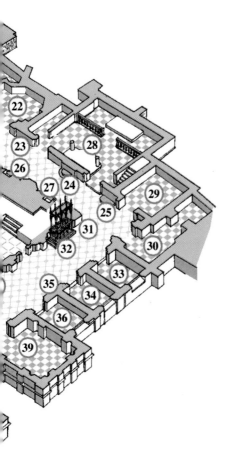

*We enter the cathedral from the west and begin the tour in the nave. Then we move on to other parts of the church, following the route on the plan. The numbers in the text correspond to the numbers in the plan. Major features which should not be missed are marked with yellow circles.*

**1**
## The nave

Its walls are faced with limestone. Their lower part is made of richly moulded arched arcades, and in their upper part, above the cornice, are windows with late-19th – century tracery (designed by Sławomir Odrzywolski), and niches with the original Gothic tracery of 1346-1364. Above the west entrance is an octagonal rose window. Along the walls and pillars up to the cross-ribbed vault run numerous shafts, interrupted by niches with the wooden **figures of the Fathers of the Church**: SS Ambrose, Jerome and Gregory (late 15th c., workshop of Wit Stwosz/Veit Stoss), and Augustine (1900, by Zygmunt Langman). On the keystones in the vault are painted the arms of the Kingdom of Poland and the Princes of Cuiavia, and the hierogram of Christ. The window to the left of the organ has an Art Nouveau stained glass with *St Casimir* (1917, by Józef Mehoffer, commissioned by Eustachy

Chronowski). In some window niches can be seen **paintings** from 1616-1617 (by Jakub Troszel and Tobiasz Tereskiewicz), which depict Christ the Saviour, the Virgin Mary and SS John the Evangelist and John the Baptist. They are remains of the paintings which once decorated the entire nave. Above the arcades hang the mid-17th – century tapestries (workshop of Jacob van Zeunen in Brussels), showing the scenes from the life of Patriarch Jacob. They are part of the eight tapestries given to the cathedral by Bishop Jan Małachowski. On the Baroque **choir loft** is the **organ** (1756-1758), topped with the figures of King David, St Damasus and Bishop Marcin Szyszkowski, who provided funds for the cathedral vocal and music band, founded in 1619 (carved by Joseph Ublaker).

**2**
## The tomb of King Ladislaus Jagiełło (d. 1434)

Gothic, made probably in the king's lifetime, attributed to the workshop from Florence or Burgundy. In 1524 King Sigismund I the Elder had it embellished with a Renaissance

---

The cathedral interior viewed from the west

**The tomb of King Ladislaus Jagiełło**

canopy (designed by Bartolomeo Berrecci). The tomb-chest of red Hungarian marble is covered by the sandstone canopy supported by eight columns. The effigy of Ladislaus Jagiełło rests supine on the tomb, with his regalia. Two lions under the king's head symbolize his power and might, while the dragon at his feet signifies evil defeated by the monarch. On the side panels are mourners (including the Archbishop of Gniezno and Bishop of Cracow), with the arms of the Kingdom of Poland and the Grand Duchy of Lithuania (shown twice), and the arms of the lands of Cuiavia and Dobrzyń, and Red Ruthenia. The plinth is decorated

**The effigy of Ladislaus Jagiełło (detail of the tomb)**

with figures of dogs and falcons (their symbolic meaning has not been explained). The panoplies decorating the canopy and medallions with the image of an emperor's triumphant entry into Rome in a chariot drawn by lions are to glorify the Polish king as an invincible warrior, whose military triumphs equal those of the Roman emperors. The tomb of Ladisalaus Jagiełło is an example of the finest and most impressive 15th – century sculpture in Central Europe.

**The effigy of King Ladislaus III**

**3**

**The effigy of Ladislaus III, King of Poland and Hungary (d. 1444)**

Made in 1906 (carved in Rome by Antoni Madeyski), of bronze and multicoloured marble. It commemorates the twenty-years-old monarch, who was killed in the Battle of Varna in 1444, fighting against the Turks. His body was never found. The youthful king, supine on the top of the chest-tomb, is presented as a knight and defender of Christendom, in full armour, holding the coronation sword of the Polish kings. The frieze on the side panels is composed of the arms of Poland and Hungary.

**4**
## The Altar of St Stanislaus, Bishop and Martyr

The relics of the major patron saint of Poland, following his canonization at Assisi in 1253, were placed in 1254 in the centre of the Romanesque cathedral, in a wooden coffin covered with silver sheet, funded by the Blessed Duchess Kinga. In 1626-1629, with the funds provided by Bishop Marcin Szyszkowski (and designed probably by Giovanni Trevano or Matteo Castello) the present **shrine** was erected, in the form of a cupola-topped canopy made of black and pink marble, and gilded bronze and wood. The statues at the top of the pillars are those of SS Stanislaus, Adalbert, Wenceslas, Florian, Casimir, Hyacinth, Sigismund and Ignatius Loyola. At the base of the cupola are the figures of the Four Evangelists. Other sculptures are the figures of seraphim and angels, and the cartouches with the arms of the founder. The cupola interior is covered with polychromy with the personified Four Cardinal Virtues (Fortitude, Prudence, Justice and Temperance). Under the canopy, on the plinth of red marble, is the Baroque **reliquary of St Stanislaus**, made in Gdańsk (1669-1671, workshop of Peter van der Rennen), of silver bequeathed by Bishop Piotr Gembicki. It has the form of a coffin, supported by four angels, and decorated at the top by the arms of the Saint and the bishop's insignia held by a pair of cherubs. The sides of the reliquary are decorated with twelve medallions (made by Iacob Iäger I or II, in Augsburg), showing scenes from the life of St Stanislaus, his martyrdom and the miracles he worked after his death (including the Polish victory over the Teutonic Knights at Grunwald). The present reliquary replaced the silver sarcophagus, commissioned by King Sigismund III in Augsburg and presented to the Cathedral by his son Ladislaus IV in 1633, which was plundered by the Swedes in 1667. To the right of the altar is the bronze **candlestick** with scenes from Christ's life, presented by the German bishops in 1980), and the **votive candle**, donated by Pope John Paul II, who in that place, on 6th June 1979, celebrated State Mass on the 900th anniversary of St Stanislaus' martyrdom. Silver lamps have always been burning at the Martyr's coffin; the present ones were made in 1805 (the central one, donated by Princess Izabela Czartoryska, neé Fleming) and 1900 (the two lateral ones, founded by Cardinal Jan Puzyna and designed by Stanisław Barabasz).

The altar of St Stanislaus is one of the finest works of early-Baroque architecture in Poland from the 1st half of the 17th c. The tomb of the patron saint of the Kingdom of Poland has functioned for centuries as the „Altar of Poland", the place where supplicatory prayers have been said for the prosperity of the nation and the state, and thanksgiving has been made for success in war and peace. In honour of St Stanislaus, many banners and trophies were laid at his tomb as votive offerings for Polish military victories. They included the banners of the Teutonic Knights captured at the Battle of Grunwald (15th July 1410) and a Turkish banner captured at the Battle of Vienna (12th September 1683). The donation of that banner by King John III Sobieski is commemorated by a marble slab in the transept, to the right of the shrine. Also, in the memorable years 1980-1981 the banners of the „Solidarity" Trade Union were blessed in this place.

## 5-8
## The monuments of the Bishops of Cracow

Placed on the pillars which surround the altar of St Stanislaus, made of black marble, with the busts of the bishops of gilded bronze. Three of them, similar but with some different details, commemorate Marcin Szyszkowski,

**The coffin of St Stanislaus**

A stained glass window in the transept

d.1630 (designed by Giovanni Trevano), Jan Małachowski, d. 1699 (commissioned by himself in 1693), and Kazimierz Łubieński, d. 1719 (designed by Kacper Bażanka?). The fourth statue, different in design, was commissioned by Piotr Gembicki (d. 1657) in his lifetime (designed 1654 by Giovanni Battista Gisleni, the bust by Giovanni Francesco Rossi).

**A stained glass window
in the transept**

**9**
**Stained glass windows in
the transept**

Designed in the Art Nouveau style (1909-19120 by Józef Mehoffer, they show *Christ the Sorrowful* and *Our Lady the Doleful* (founded by Józef Erazm Jerzmanowski), and *The Genii of Suffering*.

**10**
**The presbytery**

Its walls are similarly designed as the walls in the nave, yet their upper part is faced with sandstone, while the lower brick part is decorated with a dark-brick design. The windows had medieval stained glass until the early 17th c. Now the windows and niches have late-19th – century tracery (designed by Sławomir Odrzywolski). In the vault are keystones with reliefs showing Christ the King adored by two angels holding a thurible and a candle, as well as the patron saints of the cathedral, Stanislaus and Wenceslas, and the arms of Bishop Jan Grot (under whom the construction of the presbytery was completed). Originally, the vault had a polychromy commissioned by Casimir the Great, which imitated the sky with golden stars, and the walls were covered with paintings showing figures of saints. To the left of the High Altar are the **remains of the Gothic polychromy** (late 14th c.) with the figure of John the Evangelist. The angels holding the instruments of the Passion in the niches of the south wall were painted in 1617 (by Jakub Troszel and Tobiasz Tereskiewicz). The Baroque **High Altar**, where the kings of Poland were crowned, was commissioned by Bishop Piotr Gembicki c. 1650 (designed by Giovanni Battista Gisleni). It is made of wood and gilded, with the painting showing Christ Crucified, and with the figure of the Resurrected Christ on top, the symbol of triumph over death and Satan. To the right of the altar is the Baroque **Bishop's throne** (c. mid-17th c.), with the arms of Bishop Piotr Gembicki and the figures of SS Peter and Paul. Above the throne is the **canopy**, made probably for the coronation of Augustus III Wettin and his wife Maria Josepha (17th January 1734). Opposite the throne is the bronze **bust of Cardinal Adam Stefan Sapieha**, (d. 1951) from 1926 the first Metropolitan Archbishop of Cracow (1967, by Jadwiga Horodyska). Between the two flights of steps leading to the altar is the Gothic and Renaissance **tomb of Cardinal Frederick Jagiellon**, Archbishop of Gniezno and Bishop of Cracow, d. 1503 (by Peter Vischer in Nuremberg, 1510). The top brass slab shows the engraved figure of the Cardinal standing on a lion, within a niche with the small figures of SS Stanislaus and Adalbert. The front panel has a relief with the kneeling Cardinal, commended to Our Lady, seated on a throne, by St Stanislaus, who stands behind him with Piotrowin, the man he brought back to life. The throne is flanked by angels holding the arms with the White Eagle, and by putti. The tomb of Cardinal Frederick is among the finest works made by the Vischer workshop in Nuremberg, which often worked for the Polish Church and secular elite in the early 16th c. The inscription on the slab to the left of the steps commemorates the **original burial site of St Queen Jadwiga** (d. 1399), who was interred in front of the High Altar; her remains were transferred to the new sarcophagus in 1949. At the presbytery walls are the Mannerist **stalls** for the canons (1614-1620, by Jan Szabura), their backs and canopies reconstructed in 1901 (designed by Sławomir Odrzywolski). Above the stalls are **verdures** (tapestries showing forest landscapes), made in Holland (1658-1679, Delft?), and commissioned by Bishop Andrzej Trzebicki, with the Swan arms. On the walls on both sides of the presbytery, above small marble gates (1604-1605, by Samuel Świętkowicz), are **cartouches** (1616, by Jan Szabura), which were originally placed on the keystones in the presbytery vault, with the arms: the White Eagle with the Vasa Sheaf on its breast, the arms of the Cathedral Chapter (Three Crowns), the arms of Bishop Piotr Tylicki and the arms of Pope Paul V. A later cartouche with the Swan arms was once displayed on the vault of the north arm of the ambulatory, raised to the present height by Bishop Andrzej Trzebicki.

---

**State Mass at the High Altar →**

**The effigy of Ladislaus the Short (detail of the tomb)**

**11**
## The sarcophagus of King Ladislaus the Short (d. 1333).

Founded by his son and successor, Casimir the Great, it is the earliest royal tomb in Cracow Cathedral. A Gothic stone tomb-chest, with the supine effigy of the king on top, it displays the figures of mourners in funeral procession (clergy, nobles, and weepers) on the side panels. The present Neo-Gothic **canopy** (1900-1903, designed by Sławomir Odrzywolski), which replaced the original one (dismantled probably in the 17th c.) is decorated with the arms of the lands of the Kingdom of Poland in the reign of the king, and with the figures of saintly knights and kings.

The canopy arcades are ornamented with the Art Nouveau grille made of branches with leaves and flowers. There is a story connected with the tomb of Ladislaus the Short - the ruler who in his struggle for power several times captured and lost the city of Cracow, and finally gained the Crown of Poland. In 1655, after the Swedish troops had captured Cracow, the triumphant Swedish king, Charles Gustavus, visiting the cathedral, heard the story of King Ladislaus and declared arrogantly that the then king of Poland, John Casimir, would never return to Cracow. His guide, Fr Szymon Starowolski, replied: *Fortuna variabilis, Deus mirabilis (Fortune is changeable, and God works miracles).*

**The tomb of King Ladislaus the Short**

*Through the sacristy we enter the Sigismund Tower, then exit it through the former St Nicholas' Chapel and return to the cathedral. In winter visitors return by the same route, so after reaching the sacristy they should pass to the former St Nicholas' Chapel and continue the tour with the guidebook.*

## 12
### The sacristy (former St Margaret's Chapel)

Built in 1320-1322 by Bishop Nanker as the first chapel in the Gothic cathedral under construction, it soon began to function as a sacristy. Originally its east end was polygonal, but in the 15th c. it was extended by one rectangular bay. Its Gothic vault has reliefs on its **keystones**, showing the figures of SS Margaret and Michael the Archangel. On the walls are numerous **paintings** (17th-20th c.), including *The Martyrdom of St Adalbert*, 1754, and *St Casimir*, 1758, by Tadeusz Kuntze, painted in Rome, and *The Vision of the Blessed Vincent Kadłubek*, 1767, by Salvatore Monosilio, which were once in the altars removed from the nave in the early 20th c. Other remarkable pictures include *Madonna and Chid* (Italy, 17th c.), *Tobias Restoring Sight to His Father* (a 17th – century copy of the painting by Domenico Fetti), and *St Mary Magdalen* (by Jan Styka, 1885) from the dismantled altar in the Zebrzydowski Chapel.

## 13
### The Sigismund Tower

Inside it, on the 16th – century wooden structure, hang the largest cathedral bells (in the order the visitors approach them):

1. „**Urban**", 1460, founded by the Cracow Chapter and Jakub of Sienno, Prepositor of Gniezno and Cracow.

2. „**Cardinal**", 1455, commissioned by Cardinal Zbigniew Oleśnicki.

3. „**Sigismund**", **1520, the largest bell in Poland**, founded by King Sigismund I the Elder, cast in Cracow by the bellfounder Hans Beham of Nuremberg. Decorated with the figures of SS Stanislaus and Sigismund, it weighs c. 11 tons, its diameter is 260 cm, and its heart weighs 350 kg. It is sounded only on major church and national feast days, and to celebrate extraordinary historical events.

4. **The bell of 1751**, cast in Cracow by Jan Weidner and Samuel Scholtz.

5. „**Half-Sigismund**", 1463, founded by Jan Tęczyński, Castellan of Cracow.

The „Sigismund" Bell

**The Crypt of the National Poets**

**14**
**The former St Nicholas' Chapel**
Originally Gothic, after the rebuilding in 1775 (according to the design by Dominik Puck) it was transformed into a vestibule with the **stairs leading to the Chapterhouse**.

**15**
**The Chapel of St Thomas the Apostle and Our Lady of the Snows (Maciejowski's Chapel)**
The original Gothic structure (late 14th c., founded by Bishop Florian of Mokrsko) was replaced in the mid-16th c. by the Renaissance domed mausoleum of Bishop Samuel Maciejowski (d. 1550), commemorated by the **tomb** of sandstone and red marble (1552, workshop of Giovanni Maria Mosca, known as Padovano). In the late-Baroque **altar** of black marble (3rd quarter of the 18th c., designed by Francesco Placidi?) is one of the oldest Polish copies (early 17th c.) of Our *Lady of the Snows* in Rome. During the restoration works in 1905-1908 (designed by Zygmunt Hendel, financed by Fr Teofil Midowicz) the **present painting decoration** of the dome was executed, showing the scenes from the life of Mary and the legend of the picture of Our Lady of the Snows (by Aleksander Borawski); at the same time the bronze **grille** at the entrance was made, with the figures of angels and Madonna and Child, with Wawel in the background (designed by Sławomir Odrzywolski).

## 16
## The Crypt of the National Poets

Made in 1890 when the remains of Adam Mickiewicz (d. 1855) were transferred from Paris and placed in a marble **sarcophagus** with the poet's bust in a medallion (designed by Sławomir Odrzywolski, carved by Stanisław Roman Lewandowski). In 1927 the remains of Juliusz Słowacki (d. 1849) were brought from Paris and buried there in a modernist **sarcophagus** (designed by Adolf Szyszko-Bohusz). In the marble **urn** in the niche at the end of the crypt is the earth from the grave of Słowacki's mother, Salomea Bécu, buried in Krzemieniec. Above the altar mensa is the mosaic showing **Our Lady of the Pointed Gate**, the patroness of Lithuania (by the workshop of Antonio Salvati in Venice). The burial in the crypt in Wawel Cathedral of the greatest Polish Romantic poets, who provided spiritual support to the Polish nation, deprived of its own state, was a significant act, as it transformed Cracow Cathedral into the National Pantheon, the resting place not only of kings and military heroes, but also of spiritual leaders ("kings of the spirit"). In 1993 at the crypt entrance was placed the bronze **memorial to Cyprian Kamil Norwid** (d. 1883), another great poet (by Czesław Dźwigaj).

## 17
**The plaque showing King John III Sobieski after his victory over the Turks at Vienna (12th September 1683)**

A smaller-size copy of the painting by Jan Matejko on the 200th anniversary of the battle, which was presented by the painter to Pope Leon XIII in 1883 (exhibited in the Vatican Pinacotheca). Founded by Count Artur Potocki, it was wrought in silver by the eminent goldsmith Józef Hakowski in Cracow (1888). It was originally designed to decorate the antependium of the High Altar in the Cathedral, but in 1901 was placed in a wall (designed by Sławomir Odrzywolski), with the arms of Poland and the victorious king.

## 18
## The Chapel of SS Matthew and Matthias (the Lipski Chapel)

Originally Gothic (14th c.), twice rebuilt (1631-1633 and 1743-1746 (designed by Francesco Placidi). To the left of the entrance is the early-Baroque **tomb of Bishop Andrzej Lipski** (d. 1631), a survival of the first reconstruction, made of black marble and alabaster, with the reclining figure of the bishop on top, and with the figures of Madonna and Child, the Resurrected Christ and SS Andrew and John the Baptist. The present late-Baroque character of the chapel is the result of the second reconstruction, with its **black marble decoration** (architectural

composition of the walls, the portal, altar and monument), and **polychromy**. Most typical of the late Baroque is the coulisse framing of the **altar** made of columns (the altar contains the painting *St Matthew* by Szymon Czechowicz?), and lighting provided by hidden windows. The **monument of Cardinal Jan Aleksander Lipski** (d. 1746) on the east wall is shaped as an elaborate catafalque (*castrum doloris*) with a coffin, the Cardinal's bust in a medallion, allegorical figures (*Prudence and Fortitude*), coats of arms, and the Angel of Glory raising the curtain which separates the temporal and eternal realities. At the entrance is the Rococo iron grille with the eagles holding the Lipski family arms. The chapel is among the finest examples of late-Baroque architecture in Poland.

**19**

**The Chapel of St. Laurence (Skotnicki's Chapel, Skarszewski's Chapel)**
Founded in 1339 by Jarosław Bogoria Skotnicki, Archdeacon of Cracow (later Archbishop of Gniezno), and thoroughly rebuilt in the 17th and 18th c. In the late-Baroque **altar** of 1761 (designed by Francesco Placidi?) are two paintings: *The Adoration of the Shepherds* and *St Peter the Apostle* (by Walenty Janowski). Beneath the

---

**The east arm of the ambulatory, with the altar of Lord Jesus Crucified**

**The monument of Cardinal Jan Aleksander Lipski in the Lipski Chapel**

window is the bronze **memorial tablet of Canon Stanisław Rożnowski**, cast in 1540 in Cracow by Jorg Algajer of Ulm. Opposite the altar is the sentimental neoclassical **monument to the painter Michał Skotnicki** (d. 1808), with the figure of a female mourner of white marble, seated at a broken column with an urn on top, with brushes, a palette and a lyre at her feet. Commissioned by the artist's wife Elżbieta née Laśkiewicz in 1811, the monument was made by a Florentine sculptor, Stefano Ricci, as a replica of the monument at the

Santa Croce Church in Florence. Originally it was set in a rusticated arcade flanked with Doric columns. Among numerous memorial plaques in the chapel the most remarkable is the **epitaph of Canon Stanisław Skarszewski (d. 1625)**, who rebuilt the chapel at his own expense in 1624-1625 (opposite the altar, next to the window).

**20**
**The Chapel of SS Cosmas and Damian (the Zebrzydowski Chapel)**
Originally Gothic (2nd quarter of the 14th c.), in 1562-1563 transformed into the domed Mannerist mausoleum of Bishop Andrzej Zebrzydowski, (designed by Jan Michałowicz of Urzędowo). In the 18th c. the dome and some of its decorations were dismantled. Remains of the original decoration (including the entrance and altar arcades and the window), found in the late 19th c., were used at the partial reconstruction of the chapel in 1900-1901 (designed by Sławomir Odrzywolski). To the left of the entrance is the monument of Bishop Andrzej Zebrzydowski, d. 1560 (by Jan Michałowicz of Urzędowo), made of sandstone and marble, with the effigy of the bishop resting on the top of the sarcophagus, within the elaborate Mannerist architectural composition. The tomb is among the best Mannerist works in Poland. At the east wall is the neo-Renaissance altar with the figure of the *Sacred Heart of Jesus* (1904, by Pierre Bazzanti, in Florence).

**21**
**The altar of Jesus Crucified**
Late-Baroque (1743-1746, designed by Francesco Placidi?), made of black marble; in its centre, against the background of silver sheet (1634), is the wooden **Gothic sculpture of Christ Crucified** (late 14th c.), veiled with black tulle. The figure of Christ has been worshiped for centuries as the image famed for grace received. Adoration of Christ

**The altar of Jesus Crucified**

Crucified has been accompanied here with devotion to St Queen Jadwiga, who according to the tradition inscribed on the altar predella, used to pray here frequently and experienced a mystical vision, when Jesus

**The head of Jesus Crucified (detail of the crucifix of St Queen Jadwiga)**

Crucified spoke to her. To respect this tradition, the relics of the queen, enclosed in a small bronze coffin (designed by Witold Korski), were placed in the altar mensa in 1987. The evidence of the numerous instances of grace received from Christ in the crucifix are the votive offerings placed at His feet. Particularly remarkable among them is the **stirrup of the Grand Visir Kara Mustafa**, the commander of the Turkish army defeated by the joint Christian forces at the Battle of Vienna (12th September 1683), which was presented as a trophy and thanksgiving for the victory by King John III Sobieski. The gilded stirrup, ornamented with turquoise (the original is kept in the Cathedral Treasury, the one in the altar is a copy) was accompanied with a parchment note in the king's hand: *He whose foot rested in this stirrup is defeated by the grace of God.* The custom is that in this altar, on each Friday in Lent, the relic of the Passion Nail is exhibited; it was sent to King Ladislaus Jagiełło and his wife Sophia by Pope Martin V in 1425.

## 22
## Chapel of St Catherine (Gamrat's Chapel, Grochowski's Chapel)

Built in the mid-14th c., and later (1545-1547), by order of Queen Bona Sforza, transformed into the mausoleum of Piotr Gamrat, Bishop of Cracow and Archbishop of Gniezno (the expense was covered by the Chapter). Its Renaissance decoration was commissioned to Giovanni Maria Mosca, known as Padovano, who erected the **tomb** of the archbishop (according to the wish of the queen it was modelled on the earlier tomb of Bishop Piotr Tomicki). In the rectangular niche flanked with columns is the sarcophagus with the reclining figure of the archbishop and the relief of Madonna and Child with SS Stanislaus and Adalbert. It is topped with the small figures of SS

Catherine, and Peter and Paul. The entrance is closed with a bronze Renaissance grille (c. mid-16th c.). The present early-Baroque **decoration** of the chapel, made of black marble and stucco: wall decoration, the portal, altar with the painting *Madonna and Child with St Catherine*, and the stuccoed ceiling with the Junosza arms, are the result of the later rebuilding of the chapel (c. 1649), provided for by Fr Jerzy Grochowski.

## 23-25
## The altars of St Wenceslas, St Joseph and St Hyacinth

Late-Baroque (1747 and 1759-1761, designed by Francesco Placici?), with the paintings attributed to Szymon Czechowicz. Particularly remarkable is the elaborate antependium of the altar of St Wenceslas, made of multicoloured stone, in the technique known as *pietra dura* or Florentine mosaic.

## 26-27
## Monuments of the the kings: Michael Korybut Wiśniowiecki (d. 1673) and his wife Eleonora (d. 1697), and John III Sobieski (d. 1696) and his wife Marie Casimire (d. 1716)

Erected 1753-1760 (designed by Francesco Placidi), on the initiative of Bishop Andrzej Stanisław Kostka Załuski, and financed by Prince Michał Kazimierz Radziwiłł. Late-Baroque, they imnitate elaborate catafalques; the sarcophagi rest on the shoulders

**Monuments of the Kings Michael Korybut Wiśniowiecki and John III Sobieski**

of Turkish captives and are decorated with the scenes depicting the victorious battles against the Turks fought by Jan Sobieski at Chocim (1673) and Vienna (1683). Arcades, obelisks with royal portraits in medallions, personifications of virtues, angels blowing trumpets, and panoplies provide the monuments with a triumphant flavour and glorify the late monarchs, while skulls, gravediggers' tools, a weeping angel and the Genius of Death extinguishing a torch are reminders of the transience of human life, and little gates in the plinths symbolize the transition from temporal to eternal existence.

**28**

## The Chapel of the Birth of the Virgin Mary (the Lady Chapel, Vicar Chapel, Cyborium Chapel, Bathory Chapel)

Gothic (3rd quarter of the 14th c.), with the original three-pillared vault. It was originally decorated with Byzantine wall paintings, which were destroyed in the result of transforming the chapel into the mausoleum of King Steven Bathory (d. 1586), commissioned by his wife Anne Jagiellon, and executed by the architect and sculptor Santi Gucci in 1594-1595. The **king's effigy** and the **royal stalls**, as well as some of the **paintings in the vault** (by Kacper Kurcz) have survived. The royal tomb of sandstone and red marble, with the

The interior of the Lady Chapel, with the effigy of King Steven Bathory

reclining figure of the king, enclosed within an elaborate frame with the figures of *Prudence and Fortitude*, is among the finest examples of Mannerist sculpture in Poland. The present **early-Baroque decoration** of black marble (facing on the walls, the stalls for the vicars, the gallery supported by columns, and the portals) dates back to 1647-1650 (designed by Giovanni Battista Gisleni?), when the chapel was further refurbished at the expense of Canon Wojciech Serebryski. The **altar retable** (after 1689, founded by Suffragan Bishop Mikołaj Oborski) and the **tabernacle** (1659/1660) are made of wood painted black and covered with rich silver ornaments. The entrance has a bronze grille of 1648. The chapel was once connected with the royal palace by a roofed gallery and functioned as the royal oratory.

**29**
**Chapel of St Thomas Becket (Tomicki's Chapel)**
Founded by Bishop Piotr Tomicki in 1526-1535 (designed by Bartolomeo Berrecci) on the site of a Gothic chapel (3rd quarter of the 14th c.). Renaissance, built on the square plan and domed, it was modelled on the royal Sigismund Chapel. What has survived from the original decoration of the chapel are the modest but elegant details made of sandstone: the window frames, the cornice below the dome, the shields with arms on the pendentives, the portal leading to the sacristy. What has survived from the original Renaissance altar are the **mensa** and the **painting *The Adoration of the Magi***. The present **altar retable**, surmounted with the **relief** with the torso of God the Father (2nd quarter of the 16th c.) was composed of elements of various style and time, probably as late as the 1st quarter of the 19th c. On the altar is a small silver coffin (1901, designed by Stanisław Barabasz) with the relics of the Blessed Vincent Kadłubek, Bishop of Cracow and the author of the famous *Chronicle of Poland*. The major work of art in the chapel is the **tomb** of the founder, made of sandstone and red marble in Berrecci's workshop, with the bishop's reclining figure on the sarcophagus, and the relief of Madonna and Child adored by St Peter and Tomicki. At the top are the figures of SS Peter and John the Baptist. The epitaph was composed, on Tomicki's request, by Andrzej Krzycki, eminent humanist and Latin poet. The present **Baroque portal** of black marble replaced in c. mid-17th c. the Renaissance entrance arcade. The chapel is screened with a bronze grille (c. mid-16th c.), transferred from Bishop Samuel Maciejowski's Chapel. The original grille, with the scene of the Annunciation and the figures of SS Wencelas and Florian, cast in Hans Vischer's workshop in Nuremberg, was badly damaged during the Swedish occupation of Cracow in 1702, and later removed by the order of the Chapter. The

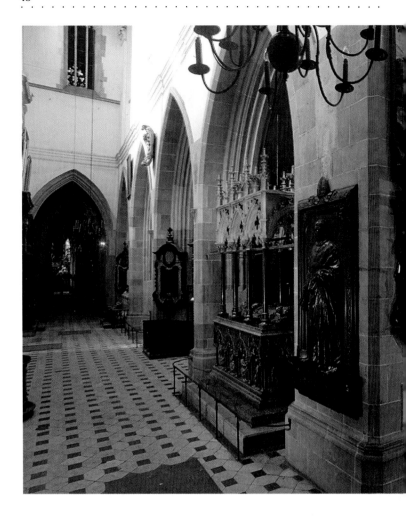

decoration of the chapel was once much more lavish - the dome and the walls were covered with polychromy in azure and gold, and the windows had stained glass with the arms of the founder, made in Flanders. The mausoleum had expensive silverware and liturgical robes made of fabrics specially commissioned from Italy. All those treasures were kept in the sacristy, in ornate cupboards.

**30**
**The Chapel of St John the Evangelist (Grot's Chapel, Załuski's Chapel)**
It was constructed after 1501, when the Gothic chapel founded in

A view to the east and south arms of the ambulatory

(designed by Francesco Placidi?), at the expense of Bishop Andrzej Stanisław Kostka Załuski. Its dome is decorated with **stuccoes** and **polychromy** which depicts The Lamb of God adored by angels. The **altar** displays the painting *The Massacre of the Innocents* (1767, by Salvatore Monosilio) and the sculpture of the Infant Jesus at the top. The monumental **portal** of black marble and stucco functions as the monument of the founder of the second refurbishing – his figure in pontifical robes can be seen above the entrance. Facing the entrance is the late-Baroque **monument**, erected in 1732-1734 (the effigy c. 1753) to commemorate Bishop Jan Grot, who died in 1346 in the opinion of saintliness and was venerated in the Cracow area. Facing the altar is the oldest object in the chapel, the Renaissance **tomb of Walenty Dembiński, Castellan of Cracow** (d. 1584). In the floor is the memorial tablet to **Jan Paweł Woronicz** (d. 1829), Bishop of Cracow and then the Primate of the Congress Kingdom of Poland, poet and excellent orator.

1344 by Bishop Jan Grot had been divided into two parts. In 1522 it was rebuilt (by Jakub Żur) as a burial chapel, the funds being provided by Chamberlain Sylwester Oarowski. The present **late-Baroque** and **Rococo** decoration is the result of its thorough refurbishing in 1758-1766

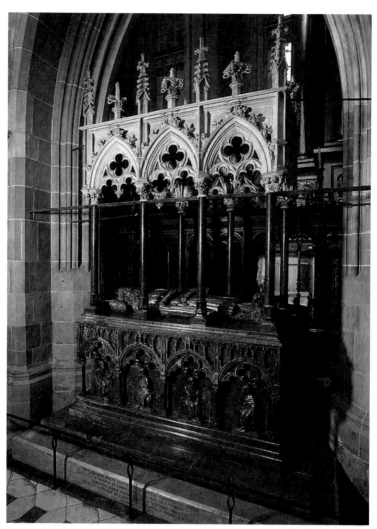

**The tomb of Casimir the Great**

**31**
**Monument of Cardinal Zbigniew Oleśnicki (d. 1455)**
Made of bronze and cast in the workshop of Casper Klemens Zumbusch in Vienna. Oleśnicki played a significant role not only in the Polish Church but also in the politics of the Kingdom of Poland. He was the first Bishop of Cracow who was raised to the dignity of the cardinal. He was buried in the presbytery, in a tomb covered once with the bronze tablet.

The effigy of Casimir the Great (detail of the tomb)

**32**
## The sarcophagus of King Casimir the Great (d. 1370)

Founded presumably by his successor, Louis of Hungary, made probably in an Austrian workshop. A Gothic tomb-chest of red Hungarian marble, it supports slender columns carrying a sandstone canopy. On the top of the tomb lies the supine effigy of the king, his feet resting on the back of a lion; on the side panels are depicted seated men - probably members of the king's council. The tomb, owing to its high artistic quality and exceptional ideological message which emphasizes the continuity of the political structure of the Kingdom of Poland (regardless of a new dynasty on the throne after the death of Casimir the Great, the last of the Piast dynasty), belongs to the finest achievements of 14th – century sculpture in Central Europe. In 1869 the tomb was opened; this event was particularly significant after the collapse of the anti-Russian January Uprising in 1863, and the ceremonial reburial of the founder of the Cracow Academy, legislator and builder of numerous castles and towns was attended by Poles from all parts of the partitioned country.

52

**The tomb of King John Albert**

**33**
**The Corpus Christi and
St Andrew's Chapel (King John
Albert's (Olbracht's) Chapel)**
Carved out of the Chapel of
St John the Evangelist after 1501,
on the orders of Queen Elizabeth of
Austria, and designed as the burial
chapel for her son, King John

Albert (d. 1501). The **king's tomb**
(1502-1505), founded by his mother
and his brother Sigismund, is
important in the history of Polish
art because of its innovatory form.
The top of the tomb-chest of red
Hungarian marble (by Jorg Huber
of Passau?), with the supine figure
of the king, is late-Gothic, while the

**The effigy of King John Albert**

architectural frame (by Francesco of Florence), in the form of an arcade modelled on ancient triumphal arches, with the arms of Poland, Lithuania and the Habsburgs, is in the new Renaissance style. The monument of John Albert is the first Renaissance tomb in Poland. The present late-Baroque decoration of the chapel: the **portal** and the **altar** with the paintings *The Martyrdom of St Andrew* (by Salvatore Monisilio) and *The Communion of St Stanislaus Kostka*, was made after 1758, from the bequest of Bishop Andrzej Stanisław Kostka Załuski. Beneath the window is the marble Renaissance **memorial** to Bishop Jan Chojeński (d. 1538), which was taken out of its original architectural frame.

**34**
**The Chapel of St John the Baptist (the Kościelecki Chapel, Zadzik's Chapel)**

Originally Gothic (c. 1350), rebuilt in the 1st quarter of the 16th c. on the orders of Crown Treasurer Andrzej Kościelecki (d. 1515), and then in 1645-1647 made into the mausoleum of Bishop Jakub Zadzik (d. 1642) by the executors of his will. Early-Baroque, its walls faced with black and pink marble, it has alabaster sculptures and a dome with rich, partly gilded **stucco decorations** and the **painted scenes** from the life of its patron saint. The **altar**, with the figures of SS John the Baptist and James the Elder, has two paintings: one of them depicts the Baptism of Christ (by Wojciech Korneli Stattler, 1836), the face of

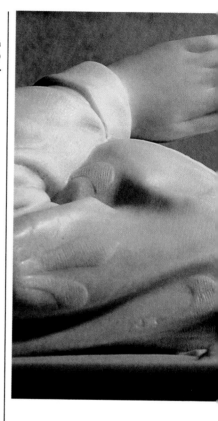

The head of Queen Jadwiga
(detail of the sarcophagus)

St John the Baptist showing the features of the poet Adam Mickiewicz; the other painting (at the top) shows Madonna and Child and St John the Baptist, the Virgin crushing the head of the dragon-Satan (1645-1647). Opposite the altar is the **tomb** with the bust of Bishop Zadzik. In the portal is the bronze **grille** with the figures of Christ the Saviour and St James the Elder.

### 35
### Monument of Cardinal Albin Dunajewski (d. 1894)

With the marble bust of the Cardinal, made by Mieczysław Zawiejski in Rome.

### 36
### The Chapel of the Immaculate Conception of the BVM (Konarski's Chapel, Szaniawski's Chapel)

Founded in 1351 by Bishop Bodzanta of Jankowo. In 1520-1521 it was transformed into the mausoleum of Bishop Jan Konarski (d.1525). His Renaissance **monument** (beneath the window) was made in the workshop of Bartolomeo Berrecci. The final refurbishing of the chapel in the late-Baroque style (the altar, tomb and portal of black and pink marble) took place in 1722-1728 (architect Kacper Bażanka).

The impressive **monument** of the sponsor of the works, Bishop Konstanty Felicjan Szaniawski (d. 1732), has his portrait in a medallion supported by the personified Glory, placed on an obelisk, which symbolizes eternity, between figures which signify the bishop's spiritual and temporal power. In the altar is the painting *St Joachim* (1834, by Rafał Hadziewicz, in Warsaw). In the floor is the bronze **plaque of Cardinal Jan Puzyna** (d. 1911).

**37**
**The funerary regalia of
St Queen Jadwiga**
The Gothic sceptre and orb
made of linden wood, originally
gilded. They were found in the first
burial place of the queen, when her
remains were transferred to the new
sarcophagus in 1949. The silver
glazed reliquary was founded from
contributions by her devotees
(1959, made by Edmund
Korosadowicz in Cracow, designed
by himself and Zbigniew
Olszakowski). Tradition explains
the modest regalia found in the
queen's tomb by the fact that she
bequeathed all her jewels for the
sake of the restoration of the
Cracow Academy (now the
Jagiellonian University).

**38**
**The monument of
St Queen Jadwiga (d. 1399)**
Founded in 1902 by Count
Karol Lanckoroński, made in
Rome by Antoni Madeyski. It is

56

a sarcophagus of white Carrarra marble, modelled on the famous tomb of Ilaria del Qareto by Jacopo della Quercia in Lucca. On the top of the tomb lies the recumbent figure of the queen, her hands clasped in prayer, a dog at her feet to symbolize fidelity. The side panels of the tomb are decorated with a frieze with eagles and the arms of the Angevin dynasty. The remains of the queen (who was originally buried in a grave at the High Altar) were deposited in the sarcophagus from 1949 to 1987.

The Sigismund Chapel, a view of the interior with the monuments of the kings Sigismund I the Elder and Sigismund Augustus

**39**

**The Chapel of the Assumption of the BVM (the Singers' Chapel, Royal or Sigismund Chapel)**

Renaissance, commissioned by King Sigismund I the Elder, built in 1519-1533 on the site of the Gothic chapel founded by Casimir the Great. It was designed by Bartolomeo Berrecci, who for executing the lavish sculptural decoration assembled a workshop consisting of Italian artists (including Giovanni Soli, Raffaello of Florence, Giovanni Cini of Siena, Niccolo Castiglione, Antonio of Fiesole, Guglielmo of Florence, Bernardini Zanobi de Gianotis, Zoan). The chapel is constructed on the square plan and covered with a dome supported by a circular drum (octagonal outside). The entrance is shaped as a triumphal arch (with the arms of Poland and Lithuania on the plinths of the pilasters) and closed with a bronze grille decorated with floral motifs and figures of putti (by Hans Vischer in Nuremberg). Above the portal are the **portraits** of Sigismund I (centre), and of Anne Jagiellon in coronation robes (left)

**The Sigismund Chapel, view towards the altarpiece**

and in widow's dress (right). The architectural composition of the walls is modelled on Roman triumphal arches. The walls are covered with sandstone reliefs with elaborate **arabesque and grotesque motifs** and mythological figures.

Each wall, except the one with the entrance, has niches with the figures of saints carved in red marble: SS Peter and Paul (east), John the Baptist and Sigismund (south) and Florian and Wenceslas (west). Above them are marble medallions with the busts of the Evangelists (east and west) and the kings of Israel, David and Solomon. At the east wall is the **altar**, a polyptych made in Nuremberg in 1531-1538, perhaps after the design by Peter Flötner The scenes on the closed wings, presenting the Passion, Death, Resurrection and Ascension of Christ, were painted by Georg Pencz. The panels seen when the altar is open show the scenes from the life of Our Lady and the figures of SS Adalbert and Stanislaus. They were wrought in silver and partly gilded by Melchior Baier, from the models cast in brass by Pankratz Labenwolf. In front of the altar stand two large bronze **candlesticks** (1534, by Hans Vischer in Nuremberg). Opposite the altar is the monument of King Sigismund I the Elder (d. 1548) and his son Sigismund Augustus (d. 1572). Made of red marble, as an arcade with the sarcophagi on two levels (Sigismund I's above, Sigismund Augustus' below); the reclining figures of the kings are presented as if in sleep, propped on an elbow, their feet crossed. Above the statue of Sigismund I is a gilded bronze **medallion** showing Madonna and Child. The original monument of Sigismund I was reworked after the death of Sigismund Augustus, whose sarcophagus, founded by his sister Anne, was carved by Santi Gucci in 1574-1575. Facing the entrance are the **royal stalls** of red marble, with two angels of gilded bronze (cast after a model by Berrecci), holding

The stalls and the effigy of Queen Anne Jagiellon in the Sigismund Chapel

a crown above the king's seat. The silver eagle on the back of the seat once decorated the roof of the dome. The stalls parapet (which was removed to the Bathory Chapel) was replaced with the effigy of Queen Anne Jagiellon (d. 1596), carved on her orders by Santi Gucci. On the pendentives supporting the dome are wooden **medallions with the arms of the Kingdom of Poland and the Grand Duchy of Lithuania** (made in the 18th c. to replace the destroyed originals). The dome is divided into coffers with rosettes, and the vault of the lantern bears the signature of the architect: BARTOLO FLORENTINO OPIFICE. The decoration of the chapel interior expresses a rich and complex ideological message, which glorified Sigismund I as

**The dome of the Vasa Chapel**

a perfect monarch (it is confirmed by the fact that King Solomon has the facial features of the founder), while the chapel is designed as a perfect temple dedicated to God by the Polish monarch. The liturgy in the chapel was celebrated by the singer priests who sang polyphonic compositions. Sigismund I and then his daughter Anne provided the chapel with rich furnishings, which included silver and gold chalices, reliquaries and other liturgical vessels (made usually in Cracow and Nuremberg), as well as rich liturgical vestments made of fine Italian fabrics. Only a small part of the furnishings has survived, now in the Cathedral Treasury and in the Czartoryski Museum. The Sigismund Chapel is one of the finest Renaissance structures in Central Europe and a crucial one in the history of Polish architecture, as it became the model for numerous domed burial chapels built by the nobility, clergy, gentry, and even townspeople. Also, the effigy of Sigismund I the Elder greatly influenced the style of Polish Renaissance and Mannerist tombs.

**40**
**The Chapel of the Immaculate Conception of the BVM (the Psalmodists' Chapel, Vasa Chapel)**
    Built in 1664-1676 (designed by Giovanni Battista Gisleni?) and founded by King John Casimir, who executed the plans of his father, Sigismund III Vasa. Its message is modelled on the mausoleum of the last Jagiellon kings (also by repeating the external form of the Sigismund Chapel). Its interior is Baroque, with the architectural and sculptural decoration of black and pink marble as well as alabaster, wood and stucco. On the walls are the **epitaphs** of the members of the royal Vasa dynasty (Sigismund III and his sons: kings Ladislaus IV and John Casimir; Charles Ferdinand, Bishop of Płock and Wrocław, John Albert, Bishop of Cracow, and Prince Alexander Charles), enclosed within elaborate frames of gilded brass.

**The dome of the Sigismund Chapel**

At the east wall is the wooden **altar** with the painting *The Assumption of the Blessed Virgin Mary* (workshop of Claude Callot?), flanked with niches containing allegorical figures. The dome is decorated with stuccoes and painted scenes from the life of Our Lady. In the black marble portal, decorated with the arms of Poland and the Vasa arms (the White Eagle with the Sheaf on its breast) is the bronze openwork gate (1673, by Michał Weinhold in Gdańsk), with images emphasizing the transitory nature of human life (skeletons crushing underfoot the attributes of all estates, the cherub blowing bubbles) and pointing to the permanence and immutability of God (the triangle, which signifies the Holy Trinity, and the circle held by cherubs, which signifies eternity). According to tradition, in the medieval Chapel of SS Peter and Paul (13th c.?), which was demolished to make room for the Vasa mausoleum, was the original tomb of St Stanislaus, and later also the tomb of Bishop Prandota (d. 1266), who was venerated in the area. In that chapel the relics of St Stanislaus' arm were kept, which were displayed to the worshippers in the arched arcade (now bricked up), which can be seen to the side of the portal.

**41**
**Memorial to Piotr Boratyński, Castellan of Bełżec (d. 1558)**
Renaissance in style, founded by his wife Barbara née Dzieduszycka.

**42**
**The Chapel of the Presentation of the BVM and St. Stephen (Doctors' Chapel, the Szafraniec Chapel)**
Situated on the ground floor of the Vicar Tower, it originally served as the chapterhouse, and in 1420 was rebuilt as the chapel of the Szafraniec family by Jan, Bishop of Cuiavia, and Piotr, Chamberlain of Cracow; it was cared for by the canons who were professors at the Cracow Academy. It was restored in 1902-1906 at the expense of Konstanty and Ferdynand Radziwiłł. Gothic, with a cross-ribbed vault. The late-Baroque **portal** and **altar** (designed by Francersco Placidi?), with the paintings: *The Vision of St John of Kanti* and *St Charles Borromeo*, 1769-1772. The Art Nouveau **polychromy** (angels on the vault, the Trumpets arms on the walls) and the **stained glass window** showing Our Lady of the Pointed Gate (which includes in the bottom part a Gothic stained glass with arms) were designed by Józef Mehoffer (1906, 1908). Facing the altar is the monument of Cardinal Jerzy Radziwiłł, d. 1600 (1904, designed by Stefan Szyller, carved by Pius Weloński). In the portal is a bronze neo-Baroque **gate** (1908, designed by Zygmunt Hendel). On the walls are the **epitaphs** of the canons of the 17th - 19th c. The most remarkable of them is the bold epitaph painting of Fr Jan Łuszczkiewicz (d. 1726).

**43**
**The bronze epitaph of Piotr Kmita the Elder, Voivode of Cracow (d. 1505)**
In the Gothic and Renaissance style, cast in Nuremberg in the workshop of Peter Vischer, it is among the finest works made in that foundry. It shows the standing figure of Kmita, in full plate armour, in his hand a lance with the Szreniawa Arms; it is flanked by the small figures of SS Peter and Paul.

**44**
**The Chapel of the Purification of the BVM (the Różyc Chapel, Padniewski's Chapel, the Potocki Chapel)**
Founded in 1381 by Bishop Zawisza of Kurozwęki, completed in 1425 by Mikołaj of Kurozwęki, Voivode of Sandomierz. After the death of Bishop Filip Padniewski it was transformed in 1572-1575 into a Mannerist domed mausoleum (designed by Jan Michałowicz of Urzędowo), and then thoroughly rebuilt in 1832-1840 with the funds provided by Zofia Potocka née Branicka (designed by Pietro Nobile). She employed local artists as well as artists from Munich and Vienna (stucco-workers Giobbe and Giovanni Axerio, sculptor Joseph Kähsman, founder Johann Georg Danninger, gilder Carl Müllner). The interior is in the neoclassical style, the walls faced with marble and imitation marble, with architectural and decorative details of gilded bronze. The dome is decorated with stuccoes (candelabra, garlands, cherub heads, rosettes); it is supported by pendentives with the figures of angels. Facing the entrance is the bronze gilded **altar** with the **painting** *Christ Crucified with SS Frances of Rome and Elizabeth of Hungary* (1630, by Giovanni Francesco Barbieri known as Guercino), purchased by Zofia Potocka in Rome. The silver **plaque** on the tabernacle door depicts Christ in the Garden of Olives (1838, by Bartolomeo Bongiovanni in Vienna). At the west wall is the Mannerist **effigy of Bishop Filip Padniewski** (d. 1572), altered by removing its side sections, carved in marble and alabaster by Jan Michałowicz of Urzędowo (c. 1575), with the epitaph inscription composed by the eminent poet Jan Kochanowski. At the east wall is the monument of Count Artur Potocki, made of white marble, with the figure of Christ standing on a pedestal with a relief showing children in prayer (1833-1834, by Bertel Thorvaldsen in Rome). The figure of Christ is a smaller replica of the famous statue in Our Lady Church (For Frue Kirke) in Copenhagen. Two marble busts, of Julia Potocka née Lubomirska and Artur Potocki, were carved by Monti after models by Thorvaldsen. The entrance is closed with an iron **grille** set in the late-Baroque **portal** of 1775.

## 45
## The Chapel of the Holy Cross and the Holy Spirit (the Jagiellon Chapel, the Holy Cross Chapel)

**The tomb of King Casimir IV**

Commissioned by King Casimir IV and his wife Elizabeth of Austria, it was built in the 3rd quarter of the 15th c. The only medieval chapel where most of its original decoration has survived. Gothic, covered with a stellar vault, with the keystones bearing the arms of Poland, Lithuania and Hungary. The walls and vault are decorated with the Byzantine **polychromy**, painted by the Ruthenian artists of the Pskov School; completed in 1470, as stated in the inscription below the window. On the vault is depicted God in His glory in heaven (symbolized by the throne surrounded with apocalyptic beasts), amidst the nine angelic choirs which worship Him. The prophets hold banderoles with quotations from the prophetic Scriptures which foretell the coming of Christ, whose Birth, Passion, Resurrection and Ascension are depicted on the chapel walls. The special role of Our Lady in the work of Salvation is emphasized by Her images (i.e. Madonna and Child enthroned above the entrance, the Virgin Mary in prayer with Jesus on Her lap, in a niche below the north window). The paintings also

**Detail of the polychromy in the Holy Cross Chapel**

**The effigy of Casimir IV
(detail of the tomb)**

show the Fathers of the Eastern
Church and the holy hermits.
Opposite the entrance was
originally the grand scene of the
Last Judgment (destroyed by the
monument constructed later). At
the east wall, flanking the
entrance, are two Gothic
**triptychs**, showing the Holy
Trinity (1467) and Our Lady the
Doleful (4th quarter of the
15th c.). Both altars are fine
examples of late-medieval
painting and sculpture produced
in Cracow. The outer panels on
the wings of the Holy Trinity
triptych have the earliest
landscapes ever used by Cracow
painters instead of gold
backgrounds. The triptych of Our
Lady the Doleful shows the
influence of Dutch painting on
Cracow artists. In the north-east
corner, at the wall with the scene
of the Dormition of the Virgin
Mary, is the **tomb of Casimir IV**
(d. 1492), made by Wit Stwosz
(Veit Stoss) c. 1492, one of the
finest works of late-Gothic
sculpture in Europe. It is carved
of spotted Salzburg marble, its
hew ranging from orange red to
dark red to grayish green. It is
a tomb-chest covered with
a canopy supported by eight
columns. On the top of the tomb
is the supine effigy of the king in
coronation robes (with the arms
of Poland and the Habsburgs
held by two lions); on the side
panels are the mourners
(representing all three estates),
holding the arms of Poland,
Lithuania, and the lands of

Dobrzyń and Cuiavia. The column capitals (one of them bearing the signature of Stwosz's co-worker Jorg Huber of Passau) depict, in the scenes taken from the Old and the New Testament, the Creation, the Fall, the constant struggle of Good and Evil in human history, and the Salvation brought about by Christ, with the Virgin Mary's help, as well as the Last Judgment as the end of history. The monument is highly expressive, a characteristic feature of the art of Wit Stwosz. In the north-west corner is the tomb of Queen Elizabeth of Austria (d. 1505), marked with a simple stone slab. Facing the entrance is the neoclassical **monument of Bishop Kajetan Sołtyk** (d. 1788), erected c. 1790 owing to Fr Michał Sołtyk

(designed by Sebastian Sierakowski?), with the standing statue of the bishop and the sarcophagus, which depicts the deportation of the bishop to Kaluga on the orders of Catherine II in 1768. Glory (an angel with a trumpet) lifts the lid of the sarcophagus and sets free the heraldic black eagle of the

Sołtyk family, while Time (a bearded old man) tries to press down the lid of the coffin. In partitioned Poland, the monument inspired strong national feelings, for the eagle emerging from the tomb was seen as a sign of Poland's resurrection. In the windows is the Art Nouveau **stained glass**

(designed by J. Mehoffer), which won an award at the Decorative Art Exhibition in Paris in 1925. It shows *The Nailing of Christ to the Cross, The Discovery of the Holy Cross by St Helena* and the allegorical Way of the Cross of humankind.

## 46
**The effigy of Piotr Kmita the Younger, Voivode of Cracow (d. 1553)**

Founded by his wife Barbara née Herburt in 1558. Renaissance in style, made of sandstone and red marble, with the standing figure of the voivode, clad in armour, in an architectural niche. It was originally placed opposite St Anthony's altar, which served the Kmita family (dismantled in 1747) and was situated in the middle arcade between the nave and the south aisle.

## 47
**The Chapel of the Holy Trinity (the Seminary Chapel, Queen Sophia's Chapel)**

Founded by Queen Sophia, the fourth wife of Ladislaus Jagiełło, and built in 1431-1433. It was originally decorated with Byzantine wall paintings (like the nearby Holy Cross Chapel) and richly furnished by the foundress

**God the Father
– detail of the polychromy on the vault in the Holy Trinity Chapel**

### The monument of Włodzimierz Potocki

with liturgical vessels and ornaments. It was repeatedly rebuilt: in 1613-1615 as the burial chapel for Bishop Piotr Tylicki, in 1836-1844 in the neo-Gothic style, with the funds provided by Anna Wąsowicz née Tyszkiewicz (designed by Franciszek Maria Lanci), and finally in 1899-1904 (designed by Sławomir Odrzywolski), with the wall painting and stained glass by Włodzimierz Tetmajer. The **polychromy** (1902-1904) shows e.g. on the vault, God the Father between the archangels who symbolize Poland and Lithuania, and surrounded by the Polish saints and blessed as well as kings, national heroes, poets and painters; on the walls is depicted the foundress, Queen Sophia being married to Ladislaus Jagiełło, and as a widow with her sons, Ladislaus and Casimir. Also, on the walls are four Marian images most venerated in Poland (Our Lady of Częstochowa, of the Pointed Gate, of Berdyczów and Kalwaria). The chapel decoration is a good example of paintings created in partitioned Poland which aimed at „uplifting the spirits" of the people, by combining religious and national motifs into an indivisible whole. In the north wall are the tombstone of **Queen Sophia** (d. 1461) and the **monument of Bishop Piotr Tylicki** (d. 1616), with a red marble relief depicting the bishop kneeling in front of Christ being nailed to the cross (1613-1614, its architectural frame c. 1900).Facing the entrance is the neoclassical **tomb of Anna Wąsowicz née Tyszkiewicz**, d. 1867, in a neo-Gothic frame (by Adam Tadolini). To the right of the entrance is the **monument of Count Włodzimierz Potocki** (d. 1812), presented in the costume of a Roman soldier; it was carved in white marble by Bertel Thorvaldsen in Rome (1820-1830), and commissioned by the Count's wife. The monument is considered to be among the finest works of neoclassical sculpture in Europe.

**48**
**The north aisle**
Covered with a net vault (1440), it played an important function in the medieval cathedral as it had the gallery (demolished in the 18th c.) where the relics of St Stanislaus' head were ceremonially displayed. It was built on top of the arcade beneath which was the Chapel of the Holy Innocents, erected in the 15th c. (some of it has survived, inaccessible to visitors). It had a balustrade, probably bearing the arms of the Kingdom of Poland; a survival of it are presumably the

arms of Cuiavia, visible above the walled-up portal (which originally led to the gallery) in the stone-faced elevation of the Clock Tower (2nd quarter of the 15th c.). In the portal is the **memorial tablet** of 1880 to the historian Jan Długosz (d. 1480).

**49**
**The monument of Bishop of Cracow Andrzej Trzebicki (d. 1679)**
Baroque, founded by his nephew, Canon Kasper Cieński, it is a rare example in Cracow of a monument with the kneeling figure of the deceased. It was originally placed at the pillar next to the tomb of Ladislaus the Short – then the statue of Trzebicki was turned in adoration to the much venerated crucifix in the nearby altar.

**50**
**The monument of Stanisław Ankwicz (d. 1840)**
Founded by his wife née Łempicka and his daughter Henrietta Ewa Sołtyk. Neoclassical (by Francesco Pozzi in Florence), with the figure of a female mourner at a broken column, and the Genius of Death extinguishing the torch of life; with reliefs referring to time passing, which is expressed in the cycle of the maturing and withering of nature (allegorical figures dancing, with a dead tree or cornfield in the background, cherubs making sheaves etc.).

*Through the Czartoryski Chapel we enter the cathedral crypts with the royal tombs, and leave the crypts by the exit leading to the court outside the cathedral.*

**51**

## The Chapel of the Passion (the Czartoryski Chapel)

Gothic, on the ground floor of the Clock Tower, covered with a stellar vault (2nd quarter of the 15th c.), with a keystone showing the arms of the Kingdom of Poland, the Chapter, and Cardinal Zbigniew Oleśnicki. After 1420 it was the chapterhouse, which was transformed into a chapel in 1873-1884 by Prince Władysław Czartoryski (architect Teofil Żebrawski), and rebuilt again in 1906 (architect Zygmunt Hendel). The **altar retable** is a neo-Gothic triptych (2nd half of the 19th c.), with late-Gothic sculptures (early 16th c.), from the altar in John Albert's Chapel, which were transferred to the church at Rudawa in the 18th c.; much damaged, they were purchased by Prince Władysław Czartoryski for his family chapel at Wawel. In the central panel is Christ Crucified, with the Virgin Mary and SS John the Evangelist, Stanislaus and Peter, who commend to Christ the kneeling King John Albert. On the wings are the Passion scenes. On the east wall is the **epitaph of Prince Władysław Czartoryski**, d. 1894 (by Antoni Madeyski in

Rome). In the entrance is the **neo-Gothic grille** with the statue of Madonna and Child (1910, designed by Z. Hendel).

**52**

## The vestibule leading to St Leonard's Crypt

It displays two **Gothic tombstones** and a **Renaissance bust from the tomb of an unknown man**, found during the restoration works in the cathedral. In 1997 the **bronze memorial plaque to politician Wincenty Witos** was placed there. Above the entrance to St Leonard's Crypt is **a fragment of a 12th-c. Romanesque lintel**, with a relief of a basilisk, found during the works in the royal crypts in the 1870s.

**53**

## St Leonard's Crypt

It is the surviving part of the Romanesque cathedral, constructed at the turn of the 11th and 12th c., and incorporated into the structure of the Gothic church. It was originally the undercroft below the west choir, built of carefully hewn limestone blocks, with details carved in sandstone. Rectangular, with a semicircular apse in its west end, divided into three aisles by columns with cube capitals, which support

St Leonard's Crypt

the groin vault resting on buttresses. In the middle, marked with a brass plaque, is the **tomb of Bishop Maurus** (d. 1118), found in 1938. The neo-Romanesque **altar** was founded by Countess Katarzyna Potocka (1876, designed by Eugene Viollet-le-Duc). On the altar step are ceramic **Romanesque floor tiles** (c. mid-13th c.), with a rich geometrical and floral ornament. On 2nd November 1946, at that altar Fr Karol Wojtyła, now Pope John Paul II, celebrated his first Mass. Along the walls are the sarcophagi of the Polish kings, queens and national heroes. At the south wall are: the neo-Baroque sarcophagus of Michael Korybut Wiśniowiecki (d. 1673) [**a**], founded in 1858 by the Austrian Emperor Francis Joseph (designed by Teofil Żebrawski), and the neoclassical sarcophagus of Marie Casimire, wife of John III Sobieski (d. 1716) [**b**], founded in 1840 by the Austrian Emperor Ferdinand I (by Karol Ceptowski). At the east wall is the neoclassical sarcophagus of John III Sobieski (d. 1696) [**c**], founded by King Stanislas Augustus Poniatowski in 1783, on the centenary of the victorious battle with the Turks at Vienna (designed by Jan Christian Kamsetzer). Next to it is the modern (1981, designed by Małgorzata and Janusz Gawłowski) sarcophagus made of one block of Silesian marble, of General Władysław Sikorski (d. 1943) [**d**],Prime Minister of the Polish Government in Exile during World War II. At the north wall are two neoclassical sargophagi: of Prince Józef Poniatowski [**e**] (founded by his sister, Maria Tyszkiewicz, 1830, by Ferdynand Kuhn), Minister of War of the Duchy of Warsaw and Marshal of France, who was fell in the Battle of Leipzig in 1813; and of Tadeusz Kościuszko [**f**] (1818, by Parys Filippi, designed by Franciszek Maria Lanci), the leader of the Insurrection in 1794, and a hero of the American Revolutionary War (d. 1817). Nearby in the wall is the bronze plaque founded by the US Congress, to commemorate Kościuszko on the bicentenary of the Battle of Saratoga (1777).

**54**
**The Crypt of King Stephen Bathory (d. 1586)**
    The Renaissance polychrome tin sarcophagus (1587, by Daniel Gieseler I or II, in Gdańsk) is decorated with the images of rulers who personify virtues and vices. Originally, it had at the top the painted portrait of the king (now in the Cathedral Museum).

**55**
**The Crypt of King Ladislaus IV (d. 1648) and Queen Cecilia Renata (d. 1644)**
    The Baroque sarcophagi of the king [**g**] and his first wife [**h**], made of gilded copper (by Johann Christian Bierpffaf) are richly decorated. The king's coffin bears the arms of Poland, Lithuania, Sweden and Gotland, and the

scenes: *The Triumph of Ladislaus IV over Abasi, Basha of Vidin, in 1633* and *The Surrender of Sheyn at Smolensk in 1634*. The queen's sarcophagus has the arms of Poland and Lithuania, Sweden, the Vasa and the Habsburg dynasties, and the Old Testament scenes: *Esther in front of Ahasuerus* and *The Visit of the Queen of Sheba to Solomon*. Next to the king's sarcophagus is the coffin of his son, Sigismund Casimir (d. 1647) [**i**], and next to the queen's one is the small coffin of her daughter, Maria Anna Isabella (d. 1642) [**j**].

## 56
## The crypt under the south arm of the ambulatory

Near the grille are the Mannerist tin sarcophagi of King Sigismund Augustus (d. 1572) [**k**] and Queen Anne Jagiellon (d.1596) [**l**], both made in Gdańsk and originally gilded and painted. Highly remarkable is the decoration of the coffin of Sigismund Augustus, with the personified senses, dormant in the result of death, and the immortal soul. Further on are the sarcophagi: of Anne of Austria, first wife of Sigismund III Vasa (d. 1598) [**q**]; Prince Alexander Charles, son of Sigismund III Vasa (d. 1634) [**m**]; Barbara Zapolya, first wife of Sigismund I the Elder (d. 1515) [**n**]; Princess Anna Maria, daughter of Sigismund III (d. 1600) [**o**]; and at the end of the crypt, King Augustus the Strong (d. 1733) [**p**].

Among the coffins is the glazed Baroque reliquary with the small coffin which contains some of the ashes of King Stanislas Leszczyński (d. 1766) [**r**].

## 57
## The crypt under the Sigismund Chapel

It contains the Renaissance stone sarcophagus of King Sigismund I the Elder (d. 1548), designed by Bartolomeo Berrecci, adorned with the king's bust in a roundel and an epitaph inscription. The sarcophagus contains also the remains of the king's son, Albert (d. 1527).

## 58
## The crypt under the Vasa Chapel

It contains the tin, copper and stone sarcophagi of the members of the Vasa dynasty: King Sigismund III (d. 1632) [**s**]; his second wife Constance of Austria (d. 1631) [**t**]; their son John Albert, Bishop of Cracow and Cardinal (d. 1634) [**u**]; King John Casimir (d. 1672) [**w**]; his wife Marie Louise Gonzaga (d. 1667) [**z**]; and their son John Sigismund (d. 1652) [**v**]. The tin sarcophagi of Sigismund III and Constance of Austria are very fine works of the casting art (made probably in Gdańsk). Particularly richly adorned is the king's coffin, with the scenes showing his victorious campaigns, and the figures of biblical kings and heroes, and with the personified virtues. In a wall niche is the urn with the entrails of John Casimir.

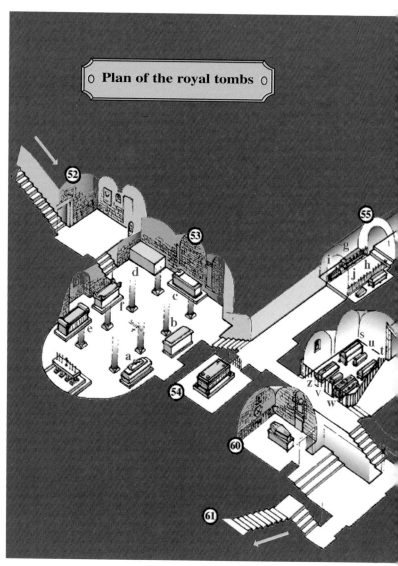

**Plan of the royal tombs**

52. Vestibule
53. St Leonard's Crypt, with the sarcophagi of: Michael Korybut Wiśniowiecki [a], Marie Casimire [b], John III Sobieski [c], General Władysław Sikorski [d], Prince Józef Poniatowski [e], Tadeusz Kościuszko [f].
54. Crypt of King Stephen Bathory
55. Crypt with the coffins of Ladislaus IV Vasa [g], Cecilia Renata [h], Sigismund Casimir [i], and

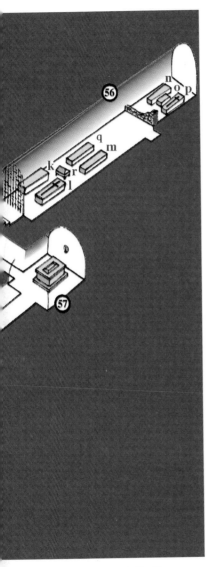

Barbara Zapolya [n], Augustus the Strong [o], Anna Maria [p], Stanislas Leszczyński [r].

57. Crypt under the Sigismund Chapel, with the sarcophagus of Sigismund I the Elder.

58. Crypt under the Vasa Chapel, with the sarcophagi of: Sigismund III Vasa [s], Constance of Austria [t], Bishop John Albert Vasa [u], John Casimir [w], Marie Louise Gonzaga [z], John Sigismund [v].

Maria Anna Isabella [j].

56. Crypt under the south arm of the ambulatory with the sarcophagi of: Sigismund Augustus [k], Anne Jagiellon [l]. Anne of Austria [q], Alexander Charles [m],

59. The plaque commemorating the Polish officers murdered at Katyn Forest.

60. Crypt of Marshal Józef Piłsudski.

61. State entrance to the royal tombs

## 59
### The vestibule leading to Piłsudski's Crypt

In a wall niche is the bronze urn with the earth from Katyn Forest, where Polish officers, prisoners of war, were shot by the NKVD in 1940. Below is the memorial plaque (1990, designed by Józef Nowakowski).

## 60
### The Crypt of Marshal Józef Piłsudski (d. 1935)

Romanesque, (with the reconstructed vault), situated on the lowest storey in the Vicar Tower. In 1936 it was furnished, together with the vestibule (designed by Adolf Szyszko-Bohusz), as the mausoleum of the first Marshal of the independent Republic of Poland and the Chief of State, Józef Piłsudski (d. 1935); his remains were placed in its centre, in a modernist brass sarcophagus. The numerous metal wreaths and plaques on the walls, founded by various army regiments, and public and veteran organizations, are a convincing evidence of the great respect Marshal Piłsudski has enjoyed in Polish society. Above the coffin is the image of Our Lady of the Pointed Gate, and in the niche (formerly the Romanesque entrance to the crypt), is the clay urn with the

earth from the grave of Piłsudski's mother at the cemetery in Vilnius (where his heart was deposited). In the entrance to the crypt is the grille with the arms of Poland and Lithuania, and the arms of Piłsudski.

## 61
### The state entrance to the royal tombs

Built in 1937 (designed by Adolf Szyszko-Bohusz). Covered with a canopy supported by nephrite columns from the demolished Orthodox church at Saxon Square (Plac Saski) in Warsaw, with the plinth from the dismantled monument of Bismarck, with metal details cast from captured Austrian guns. The canopy, which symbolizes the three partitioned sections of the country united in the reborn Polish state, bears a significant Latin inscription: „CORPORA DORMIUNT VIGILANT ANIMAE" (the bodies are asleep, the souls are awake).

**The Crypt of Marshal Józef Piłsudski**

LITURGY AT CRACOW CATHEDRAL

**Metropolitan Archbishop Franciszek Macharski
on the throne of the Bishops of Cracow**

**State pontifical Mass at the High Altar**

**Blessing of the Holy Oils on Maundy Thursday**

**Prayers at the sarcophagus of Casimir IV, on the 500th anniversary of the king's death (1992)**

**Pontifical Mass at the Altar of Poland**

**Papal blessing at the end of the Mass celebrated in St Leonard's Crypt
(9th June 1997)**

Pope John Paul II praying at the crucifix and the relics of St Jadwiga (1991)